# I Don't Want to Bully Anymore

## A Young Person's Guide for the Bully and the Bullied

# June Rousso, Ph.D.

Copyright © 2019 by June Rousso. All rights reserved.
This book, or parts thereof may not be reproduced in any form without permission from the publisher except for brief excerpts used for reviews.

Illustrator-Maima Adiputri

ISBN 13: 978-1-937985-52-3
ISBN 10: 1-937985-52-0

Printed in the U.S.A.

june.rousso23@gmail.com
www.junerousso.com

The 24-character strengths in this poem are the VIA Classification of Character Strengths. For more information on the VIA character strengths visit: www.viacharacter.org VIA Classification ©Copyright 2004-2018, VIA Institute on Character. All Rights Reserved. Used with Permission.

# DEDICATION

To my father, whose inspiration has always guided me.

# INTRODUCTION

Who hasn't been bullied from time to time? Unfortunately, some bullies do not give up. And it hurts, whether from physical bullying or an emotional bruise from hurtful words. We are told to ignore the bully, but sometimes it's hard to do in an age where a large audience can now witness and encourage cyber-bullying.

For anyone who has ever thought of bullying or has bullied others, take a look within yourself, to your own unique character strengths. You have them. Becoming aware of and accepting your character strengths will help you to feel good about yourself, avoiding the urge to put others down.

And for the victim of bullying, looking to your character strengths is a reminder of who you really are and not someone perceived through the eyes of a bully. When we do not like ourselves, we are more likely to accept those hurtful words because we believe in what the bully has to say. All the more reason to look within to search for our character strengths. They're there in each and every one of us.

What are character strengths some of you will ask? Through extensive research the VIA Institute on Character has discovered twenty-four character strengths that we all share. Becoming acquainted with them and learning which ones are unique to you is one way to deter bullying. There is no reason to bully when you find the good in yourself and have an eye toward the strengths in others.

And now a few words from the bully and an introduction to character strengths.

# LETTER FROM THE BULLY

Dear Victim,

I started thinking about my behavior, and I have to admit, I am confused why I bully. Once I pick my target, I get so focused that I feel something takes over my emotions. Sometimes I can't even remember why I choose you. But after I bully you, I never feel as good as I thought I would. Whether I call you names, or write something nasty on social media, or steal your lunch money, deep down inside I never feel good.

Part of me is proud that I am called a bully. People know my name, and a lot of people are afraid of me. That makes me feel powerful. I can do almost anything to you. I can call you names, laugh in your face, make fun of you in front of other people. I can push you, invade your personal space, and make you feel scared. And don't even show me you're afraid because that makes me feel more powerful.

But at the end of the day when I think about my behavior, I'm not happy. I don't understand why I bully. I really don't. Sometimes I start without thinking. I have promised myself I would change, but it's hard. I wish there were a way for me to stop being a bully.

Please understand, I don't want to bully anymore.

*The Bully*

# ODE TO A BULLY

There once was a boy who walked my way,
and put down everything that I had to say.
He called me dumb, a fool, and a goof,
always acting like he had all the proof.

Sadly, I took him at his word,
believing everything I ever heard.
Whatever the bully had to say,
would end up ruining the rest of my day.

The bully made me feel hurt and mad inside,
all I wanted to do was run away and hide.
Racing home and into my bed,
I tried to forget the mean words that he said.

But trying to shut out the words did not work,
I truly began to believe that I was a jerk.
Words have a funny way of sticking like glue,
once they take hold, you believe them to be true.

I could not push his words away, even if I tried,
they filled up all of my thoughts - far and wide.
But then one day I wondered if the bully knew me all that well,
and then I thought - not very much that I could tell.

After all, people have been told that I am kind,
and have an imaginative and curious mind.
Loving learning every day,
not letting my frustrations get in the way.

I know how to put my mind to work and to keep trying,
I value telling the truth and do not like lying.
Acting on my beliefs means so much to me,
and not judging others, just letting them be.

I'm funny and like making people laugh just to feel good,
I do most- yes most- of what I think I should.
I don't pick on people because it can hurt so much inside,
I am a true friend - always listening and trying to guide.

This may sound like bragging, but it is really not,
it is a way to remind myself of all that I have got.
And bully, why not make a list of all that is good in you?
Then you may come to like yourself and people around you, too.

You will do yourself and the world a favor,
finding good times and friends to savor.
That's a lot better than putting others down.
No one will like or love you that way,
and you will be the one truly sad at the end of the day!

# VIA CHARACTER STRENGTHS

Now that you have a taste of character strengths let's look at what the VIA research has found. Below is a list of twenty-four character strengths. Which ones are unique to you? When you are interacting with others, focus on what they do well, rather than what they do wrong. Try to always look for their character strengths.

**Appreciation of Beauty and Excellence**

- There's so much beauty in the world- inside and out- the trees, oceans, kindness, compassion – you get the point. And what one person sees as beauty, another may not, and we need to respect others for how they see the world. What beauty do you appreciate in your life? How can you add more beauty to your life?

- Excellence comes in many shapes and forms. It can be doing exceptionally well on a test, a job, or the way we attend to others when they need our help. Excellence does not have to mean perfect. None of us are perfect, and it can be a burden to strive for perfection. Describe a situation when striving for perfection became a burden. What are some ways you might strive for excellence?

## Bravery

- Many of us learn to put on a brave face or be brave and take a risk. Riding a bicycle, jumping in the ocean for the first time, facing our anxieties and fears – these are all acts of bravery. What acts of bravery can you remember that you are proud of? What acts of bravery might you consider in the future?

## Creativity

- Being creative allows us to express our true selves and come up with original ways of looking at things. People are creative in different ways- through acting, painting, writing, and just coming up with creative ideas. Don't be afraid of using your creativity. The world is waiting for you. What are some ways that you can think and act more creatively?

## Curiosity

- The world extends far and wide, present and past. Being curious is our way of expanding our knowledge and understanding of people and ourselves. Don't be afraid to ask questions. Otherwise, you will stifle your curiosity and not broaden your life experiences. What are some things that you have been curious about and how can you go about, learning more?

## Fairness

- Life can be unfair at times, but it is up to us to be fair to others. Rather than acting selfishly, look to compromise, and find decisions that everyone can live with. When we are able to compromise, life seems fair all around. Describe a unfair situation and come up with ways to reach a compromise.

**Forgiveness**

- Living with hurt and anger when people treat us unfairly can be more painful than how others have actually treated us. Forgiveness does not mean having someone who wronged us back in our lives. It can, but it also can mean forgiving, not holding onto a grudge, and nothing more. What people in your life would you like to forgive and how would you go about it? How have you felt when someone has forgiven you?

**Gratitude**

- There is so much we take for granted day in and day out. Practicing gratitude makes us feel good about ourselves and others. Think about what seem to be the little things in life that you are grateful for. How do you feel after the practice? Often what seems like the little things are much bigger and more meaningful to us than experiences that we thought meant more to us.

**Honesty**

- As children, we are taught to be honest, but there will always be situations when we lie, sometimes just to make ourselves look good in our eyes and to other people. But underneath most people do not feel good about themselves when they tell lies. They feel at their best, knowing that they are telling the truth. How do you feel telling a lie and when telling the truth? How do you feel when someone lies to you and how do you handle the situation?

**Hope**

- Hope helps to make things happen. Even if a situation feels hopeless and we have to give up for whatever reason, we can always bring hope to a new situation. With hope, we can look forward to the future and with optimism. So when times are little rough, having hope for the future can make us feel better. What do you hope for and what steps can you take to make it happen?

**Humility**

- While we may have much to be proud of in our lives, sometimes it is best not to show ourselves off to others. When we are good at what we do or who we are, we should feel secure in ourselves and not have to tout our talents. If they are there, others will see them in us. In what ways can you act with more humility? What are constructive ways to react to people when they are not humble?

**Humor**

- Life without a sense of humor can be pretty dull at times. We need to learn to laugh at ourselves and not to laugh at others at their expense. Rather than always being so serious, look for the humor in situations. Even in the worst of experiences, learning to laugh helps to soften the blow. What situations in your life could have had a dose of laughter? What present situations can you bring laughter to?

## Judgment

- Judgment is learning to be objective, to consider all sides of a situation and not make decisions based on your desires as much as the right thing to do. People often advise others based on their own needs rather than thinking through what might be good for them. It's just part of being human. What situations have you offered advice on what might have been good for you, but did not consider the needs of others?

## Kindness

- Kindness is something all people deserve, including ourselves. Being kind is not a sign of weakness. It is a sign of strength. When we are kind to others, we feel good in knowing that we brightened up someone's day even if just for a moment. Sometimes that moment makes a person's whole day. In what ways can you be kinder to yourself and other people? How do you view kindness- as a strength or a weakness?

## Leadership

- Leadership takes inner strength, being able to lead others without taking over. It involves considering the needs of others, not just what we would want for ourselves. Leadership also involves knowing when to step back and let others lead the way. When have you been able to take the lead? What obstacles have stopped you from being a leader? How can you overcome these obstacles? Are there situations in which you can let others lead?

## Love

- We do not need to love or feel loved by everyone we meet in life. To have some people to love and feel loved by is a gift. We also need to have compassion toward ourselves as a form of self-love. Sometimes people are too hard on themselves, judging perceived mistakes or weaknesses harshly, yet able to love others. In what ways can you be more loving toward yourself? How can you be more loving to others?

## Love of Learning

- Life is a journey, and we should always keep our minds open to learning. This makes the difference between a fixed mindset and a growth mindset. We can stay as we are or try new experiences, and let them shape our thoughts and feelings about the world. What are some fixed ways of thinking that you have and how can you change your views to be more open to change and growth?

## Perseverance

- When we set goals for ourselves or they are set for us, we are bound to meet obstacles. Perseverance is the strength that allows facing those obstacles and not be so discouraged by them that we give up. What major obstacles have you had to face in your life and how did you go about overcoming them? Sometimes people are impatient about reaching their goals. If this is you, how can you go about becoming more patient?

## Perspective

- Before making a decision or expressing a thought or feeling, we need to consider the points of view of others. Our thoughts and feelings at their best are shaped by how others see a situation and not just our point of view. Taking in the views of others helps in making the best decisions. Describe a situation in which a decision was made only on your thoughts and feelings? How can you work to develop perspective?

## Prudence

- Prudence involves acting with caution and thinking things through. When we take risks without considering the consequences, we are acting impulsively, not prudently, and can hurt ourselves and others along the way. What are some situations where you did not act prudently and what were some of the consequences of your actions? What are some ways that would help to develop prudence?

## Self-regulation

- Self-regulation involves discipline and self-control. So may life situations require self-regulation. Being a student or employee requires discipline as much as we need to learn to self-regulate our emotions and not over-react to situations that have upset us. What are some times when your emotions took over and how could you have handled the situation better?

## Social Intelligence

- With social intelligence we are attuned to our thoughts and feelings along with the thoughts and feelings of others. By tuning into others, we build empathy, and care for others and not just our own self-interests. The best decisions are made using thoughts and feelings, and not just relying on our logic. How could you bring feelings in more when making decisions for yourself?

## Spirituality

- The spirit in us seeks to find meaning in life rather than live a day-to-day existence. Some people search a lifetime to find meaning in life, reflecting how important meaning is to our well-being and personal satisfaction. What experiences might give you meaning in life? How can you work toward reaching your goals? How can you make some of your present experiences more meaningful?

## Teamwork

- Working as a team can be rewarding. Not only are you reaching your goals, you are helping others to reach theirs. It is only in relation to other people that we can truly grow as human beings. Teamwork does not mean that something is being taken away from us. It has the power to add to everyone's satisfaction. What situations could you change to bring in more teamwork?

**Zest**

- Life can feel hum-drum or we can approach it with excitement and energy, setting goals and looking forward to the days ahead, and always being open to new experiences. Not every day is going to be packed with zest. Life has its ups and downs. What experiences have you approached with zest? How can you work to increase zest in your life?

# ABOUT THE AUTHOR

Dr. Rousso's other books written for a child and adolescent audience stress the importance of recognizing character strengths in ourselves and spotting strengths in others. They are:

*We All Live on This Planet Together* (2017) which focuses on looking for the positive in life rather than dwelling on the negative.

*The Little Book of Character Strengths* (2018) introduces young readers to the concept of character strengths and how to apply them in their lives based upon the VIA classification.

You can learn more about June Rousso and making character strengths a central focus in guiding your thoughts and actions by visiting her website at http://junerousso.com

www.ingramcontent.com/pod-product-compliance
Lightning Source LLC
Chambersburg PA
CBHW050748110526
44591CB00002B/17